Social Skills

Simple Techniques to Manage Your Shyness, Improve Conversations, Develop Your Charisma and Make Friends In No Time

By
James W. Williams

Copyright © 2018 All rights reserved.

No part of this publication may be copied, reproduced in any format, by any means, electronic or otherwise, without prior consent from the copyright owner and publisher of this book.

James W. Williams

Table of contents

Your Free Gift 5

Introduction 7

Chapter 1: Overcoming Shyness 12

    How to Beat One-On-One Shyness 13

    How to Get Over Shyness at Work or at School 16

    How to Get Your Voice to be Heard 21

    General Suggestions on How to Overcome Shyness 23

Chapter 2: How to Improve Your Conversation Skills 26

    Keep the Flow 26

    Open Up 28

    Listen Actively 29

Chapter 3: How to Develop Your Charisma 32

    Engage Attention 32

    Affect Your Audience 34

    Making the Awkward Behavior Go Away 37

Social Skills

Closing 39

Thank you! 42

Your Free Gift

As a way of saying thanks for your purchase, I wanted to offer you a free bonus E-book called ***Bulletproof Confidence Checklist*** exclusive to the readers of this book.

To get instant access just go to:

https://theartofmastery.com/confidence/

Inside the book, you will discover:

- What is shyness & social anxiety, and the psychology behind it
- Simple yet powerful strategies for overcoming social anxiety
- Breakdown of the traits of what makes a confident person
- Traits you must DESTROY if you want to become confident

- Easy techniques you can implement TODAY to keep the conversation flowing
- Confidence checklist to ensure you're on the right path of self-development

Introduction

You could feel countless eyes staring right at you. You become immobilized. You wish the stage will open and swallow you up! How in God's name did you get yourself into this awkward situation? You open your mouth but the words won't come out. You can hear someone from the audience say "Speak up you dummy!" and your legs start to quake. You feel the bile from the pit of your belly and you rush off the stage.

Although not all of us are public speakers, I know that to some degree, you can relate with the shy and inexperienced imaginary character above that was experiencing the seemingly daunting task of his first-time on stage in front of an audience. It is not an experience to look forward to. Trust me, I know.

Interacting with people as individuals or as a group is a very difficult proposition for many people. To some, it is a very debilitating experience that they would rather avoid by all means. But for communication between humans to be effective, good social skills must be employed. After all, we as humans are social creatures with an inborn need to interact with other humans.

A lot of people suffer from shyness and lack of charisma and this directly impacts negatively on their ability to interact socially. This can result in low self-esteem and a poor self-image. You may know of a person who became socially withdrawn or is a lone wolf because of their lack of good social skills. They feel out of place when they find themselves in the midst of people or they find it extremely awkward when there is a need for them to say a simple "hello" especially to a stranger.

We may not all be introverts or excessively shy. And we may not all want to be public speakers or the center of attention in the midst of social gatherings. But we all do need good social skills in order to enjoy the company of our friends, family and even strangers. The good news is: being shy is not a death sentence. You can actually develop your social skills little by little or at a pace that is comfortable for you.

Perhaps you have read books about social skills that all sounded bogus and filled with vague tips; or maybe you are almost giving up and recoiling into your shell of timidity; or you are in search for a book that shows you the exact tips and the "how to" of becoming great with your social skills; whatever your case, this book is guaranteed to give you the boost of confidence you need to relate with people, make new and amazing friends, communicate effectively, and most importantly, give you a sense of belonging in your world.

Let me be realistic here and tell you upfront: you are not going to become great with your social skills overnight or by simply reading a book. Work is required on your part. You need to be committed to improving your skills and stick to it until you achieve your desired results.

From my experience and the experiences of millions of other people, it is certain that things happen for us in accordance with who we are; happy things search for happy people and happen to them. Amazing things look for amazing people and happen to them. Lonely, withdrawn, and unsure people... well, let's just say they aren't as happy as they know they could be. For exciting things to happen for you, you need to go out and mix up with exciting people; let their energy of excitement rub off on you. Then, exciting things can happen to you.

Lots of people have used the exact same tips and techniques I share in this book to transform their almost nonexistent social life into an amazing lifestyle donned with the right kinds of people they so desire.

It is time to put an end to that awkward feeling of social anxiety or social phobia. Take a leap into a new world of endless possibilities as you read and apply my "how to" techniques on improving your social skills.

Chapter 1: Overcoming Shyness

Obviously, the first step in improving your social skills is overcoming shyness. I mean, you don't teach a shy person how to charm others or how to make friends quickly without first showing them how to beat their shyness.

I will not bore you with some synopsis of what shyness is or the negative effect of shyness. You probably know the effect which is why you are reading this book. Everyone knows that shyness can wreck a person's chances at work, in relationships, at school, in social gatherings, and generally in relating with other people. And no one likes that uncomfortable and timid feeling shyness brings. So let's delve straight into how to overcome shyness with the proven techniques below.

How to Beat One-On-One Shyness

Having one-on-ones can trigger a lot of uncomfortable feelings for a shy person. One-on-ones can be with your boss (very disquieting), a stranger (very creepy), your in-laws (very awkward), or someone you have a crush on (very unnerving). This can quickly reflect visibly in your body: heartbeats increases, palms get sweaty, temperature increases, face flushes, you begin to fidget uncontrollably – it's almost a pitiable sight to behold!

Basically, to overcome this you need to take charge of the reactions in your body. Those reactions are your senses screaming at you to take cover because they sense you are stepping into a "danger zone." It is their way of protecting and keeping you safe. Take charge by telling your senses that you've got this under control. Here's how you do that.

1. Take deep breaths: when faced with one-on-one, take controlled and deep breaths, holding

the breaths in a bit longer than you would normally do before letting it out slowly. When you do this, you tell your nerves to calm down. It is a way of asserting your authority; making your body realize that you are in charge and they (your nervous system and its sensors) can rest easy. Breathing deeply has a way of relieving you of built up stress and anxiety. It also allows you to think more clearly.

2. Adjust your body posture: you can sniff out a shy person from a mile away by the way they carry themselves. When faced with one-on-one, don't let your head down – literally, don't! Keep your head upright and look straight ahead or at the person. Broaden your shoulders and keep your elbows and arms away from your ribs. And whatever you do, do not let your hands go into your pockets! That's a dead giveaway that you are nervous. And once your body receives this nervous signal, you can be sure it will shut down other body systems to protect you from this perceived "danger." Get a good grip of the

message your body language is passing. Adjust your posture to show confidence rather than submissiveness. Notice any tensed muscles in your body and loosen them up by tightening and relaxing them repeatedly for a few seconds. And by all means no hunching! Stand up tall or sit up (except when you choose to lean back to show confidence).

3. Shift your focus away from you: here's the thing; we all have inadequacies and flaws, but to a person having a large dose of insecurity or lack of self-confidence their attention is usually riveted on their own shortcomings. Their feeble mind continuously chatters and deafens them with loud screeches of "you are not good enough," "you can't do that," so they automatically place their focus on their perceived defects whenever they are in contact with a person whom they assume is better than them in some way. To overcome these so-called flaws of yours, shift your attention to something other than you when you are having a one-on-one. Give

your attention to your surroundings, the in and out of your controlled breaths, or any other thing aside from your weaknesses. Well, actually not any other thing really because that may distract you from conversations that may occur during your one-on-one. Basically, I will recommend that you shift your attention away from you to the other person. What are they saying? How are they carrying themselves? What can you emulate from them? Is there something you like about them? When conversing during one-on-ones, give your mind some task by allowing yourself to be curious. Let your curiosity show up in the questions you ask. This way, your mind will not be focused on you but on the other person.

How to Get Over Shyness at Work or at School

The workplace and school are two places most people (adults and young people) spend a lot of their waking hours. This means that shy persons are always in a closed community where their reputation for shyness can spread really fast. This is an added pressure to the shy person.

Okay, so how do you survive under such pressure as a shy person? How do you not cringe and drift back more into your shell? Here's how:

1. Become an expert: have you noticed how the go-to guy in the office seems to have an extra dose of self-confidence? Well, his confidence level wasn't always that way until people began tumbling over themselves to get to him because of what he can help them do. And have you noticed how the student who is good at what he or she does seem to never lack other students flocking around them? Being good at what you do whether at work or in school is a great way to help you overcome shyness because it opens you up to social interactions with the people that seek your expertise. It may appear that you are at the giving end of these interactions as you are offering something they need. But in the actual sense, it's a win-win relationship because you are equally

building your self-confidence and learning better ways to interact with people and socially integrate with your peers. It's kind of what students would refer to as a symbiotic relationship and working-class persons would call a mutually beneficial liaison. So get to work on that skill, talent, hobby, subject, course, or whatever it is you have a flair for and become really good at it. People at work or school are sure to notice and come flocking around you.

2. Deliberately put yourself forward: did I mention you have to be determined in your efforts to overcome shyness? Well, you do have to be determined. Shyness cannot be wished away; neither can you think it away. One way to show your determination is to choose to put yourself forward by participating in things that would normally scare the living daylight out of you. Offer to give a presentation in class or at work; walk up to a group of colleagues or classmates and join in the conversation; offer to host the next office or class party; just do

something, anything that being shy has kept you away from doing. Challenge your shyness. Put it on the spotlight. Yes, you may fail and falter the first few times, but that's how we all learn to walk right? You didn't just get up as an infant and began strutting about. You fell and probably banged your head a couple of times. But your determination to walk kept you going until walking became natural for you. However, I recommend that you start putting yourself forward with little baby steps. You don't want to jump into things that the failure level will be so massive that it completely shuts down whatever little zest that has begun to build up in you. Take your challenge step by step. Avoid quantum leaps.

3. Timeliness: I just said take baby steps in your fight against shyness. One way to not do that is by being late for work or class. What does being late have to do with not taking baby steps? It has everything to do with it. Here's how. Picture how you will feel as a shy person walking into the class

when lectures have already begun or walking into the conference room when the meeting is well underway: all eyes on you, right? You feel like disappearing because of the unwelcome attention. Your steps begin to falter as you walk to your seat; you get clumsy and fumble with your books or folders and stuff. You have bitten more than you can chew; you have inadvertently placed yourself on the spotlight because you did not take baby steps! Lesson: be on time. Do not give your shyness trigger more reason to shut down when you are in the presence of people.

4. Participate more: the thing is you cannot overcome shyness by avoiding social activities. Thankfully, school and work offer a good number of social activities that can help you outgrow shyness if and only if you decide to participate in such activities. Beat obscurity by stepping out of the shadows and participate in social activities. I am not suggesting that you should strive to become the prom queen or the most communicative staff of the year (although that

isn't entirely a bad goal for a shy person!), I am simply stating the obvious: become more open to take part in activities that expose you to learn how to be free with other people.

How to Get Your Voice to be Heard

Shy people are always quiet as if in a hush-hush attitude. Well, they are not hushing because they are keeping some vital secret that is capable of sending us all into extinction if exposed! No. They are quiet because most of their conversations take place in a realm that is not physical – in their head. And a large chunk of that conversation is negative chatter.

Being quiet or habitually speaking in a low tone is a sign of shyness. If you are not sure whether or not you speak with a low voice, here's a sure fire way to find out: ask someone if your voice is always low. Another way to know you speak in a low tone is if you are often asked to repeat yourself, or you are often misunderstood. If people usually have to lean towards you before they get what you are saying, you definitely are the hush-hush shy type.

To be socially active (at least to a healthy degree), you need to learn how to literally get your voice to be heard; you need to practice how to raise your voice. And this is how to do that:

1. Breathe deeply before opening your mouth to speak
2. Let your voice spring up from deep inside your belly or diaphragm (just don't be too obvious about this; it'll make you appear as if you want to puke).
3. Allow your words to form clearly and let them fall off your lips in a distinct manner.
4. Speak using a good pace; not too slowly and not in a hurriedly jumbled pace.
5. Make a habit of speaking to someone across the room; it will definitely make you speak louder.

General Suggestions on How to Overcome Shyness

Let me bring this chapter to a close by suggesting a few other simple tips for overcoming shyness.

1. Applaud yourself: your mind has a way of getting you to repeat something that gives you pleasure. When you commend yourself for the efforts (no matter how little) you put into overcoming shyness, your mind takes notice of the good feeling you get from that applause and shows you better ways of doing those actions that made you commend yourself. In other words, your mind helps you become better the next time you do that same thing or it opens you up to more opportunities to do that same thing in a better way. This is a great way to improve from being a shy person to a more outgoing person. So, get in the habit of taking a moment at the end of each day to applaud yourself for saying "hello" to a complete stranger, or for maintaining eye contact

with another person as they conversed with you, or for responding to a question in a class.

2. Practice meditation: yes, I know that meditation is a spiritual practice but it has a way of calming our minds and quieting our train of thoughts. Since shy people usually battle with negative self-talk, meditation will help to reduce these unpleasant mental talks and refocus the mind to overcome anxiety and shyness.

3. Meet physically with real humans: it is easy to confuse social media interactions with real-life human interactions. Shy people are not dumb! In fact, they are very good with words; only not spoken words. So you can be good at expressing yourself in writing especially online but that does not necessarily mean you are good at real-life socializing. Get in touch with real humans physically and interact. That is how to overcome shyness.

4. Learn conversation skills: conversation skills are part of social skills. Social skills build self-confidence. Self-confidence and shyness are far removed from each other. Learning conversion skills is a major way to help you overcome shyness. Go to social events, listen to conversations, and pick up tips about public speaking – that's how to learn conversation skills.

One quick word about public speaking: although this book does not aim to make everyone a public speaker, it is important to mention that many of the skills required to be a good public speaker are also the essential skills for being good at conversations. Thankfully, the next chapter is on how to improve your conversation skills.

Chapter 2: How to Improve Your Conversation Skills

Conversation is a way of bonding. It should be the most natural thing for social beings like humans who use words in communication. But alas! Some of us have a serious phobia for engaging in conversations. Your conversation skills definitely need improving if you are having a conversation with the following questions popping up in your head: what should I say next? Should I talk now or do I wait for him/her to speak?

Okay, so what do you do to make conversations flow naturally? Here are some awesome tips for improving your conversation skills.

Keep the Flow

Uneasy pauses are a sign of poor conversation. It shows that someone (or some people) is anxious about the interaction. To keep the conversation flowing:

1. Avoid eliciting one-word responses: "fine," or "it was great," are the kind of responses you get to the question, "how was your day?" and it ends there. But when you frame the same question like this, "what did you do today?" the person answering the question is free to talk for as long as they wish.

2. Leave out the superficial questions: to make conversations meaningful and worthwhile, don't flood your talk with superficial questions such, "do you think the weather will be great tomorrow?" Dig deeper with your questions – be up close and personal if you have to (and when the other person is comfortable with it).

3. Share so that they also want to share: remember you are having a conversation and not an interview. Flooding your conversation with question after question is still a sign of poor

conversation. Instead of only asking questions, interject direct questions by saying something about yourself or a situation that makes the other person want to also tell you about themselves or a situation. You do not limit the other person by requiring them to answer your question and stop. You give them the chance to ask you questions, share their opinion about what you have said, or share a similar story to yours.

Open Up

So, you want to create a good bond with a stranger or someone you barely know and hit it off with a great conversation; be ready to be open. The more you open up and let them know about you, the more they will flow with you and also open up to you. How then do you open up as a way of improving your conversation skill?

1. Talk about yourself: talking about yourself (not in a conceited manner) will give your listener the clue that you want to be friends with

them or you want to connect with them. Talk about your opinions, your life, and even your feelings and in turn, your listener will likely share about themselves too. Be mindful not to give out too much information too soon though.

2. Understand yourself: you cannot properly talk about yourself – your interests, opinions, beliefs, motivations, fears, etc – if you do not know them (and you will be surprised at the number of people who don't know themselves!) For your conversation to flow and bonds with others to grow stronger, there must be knowing of each other. So do your part by understanding who you are.

Listen Actively

Conversation is not just talking nonstop. In fact, too much talking shows your conversation skills need brushing up. There is a place – a huge place for listening in a conversation. Here's how to listen actively:

1. Repeat when necessary: to show the other person you are immersed in what they have shared with you, repeat what they have told you using your words, and then you can proceed to add your opinions or suggestions and even ask more questions.

2. Nod: give nods to show that you are not just hearing their words, but also paying attention to what they are saying and are tuned into them. But don't overdo it. Nodding too much show you are not paying attention but just trying to please them.

3. Clarify with questions: to show the other person that you are actively listening and following the conversation, intermittently ask clarifying questions. You could say "What precisely are you referring to when you say...." or something along that line.

4. Listen; don't bother about your response... yet: a conversation is not an inquisition so relax and listen to what the other person is saying. Thinking about your response while the other person is still talking shows you are not fully paying attention. Practice holding off responding for a few seconds after the other person has finished talking.

Chapter 3: How to Develop Your Charisma

Being good at what you do is great, however, without charisma, you probably won't excel at what you do. Countless musicians, performers, leaders, and great speakers have had the need to improve their charisma in other to become charming to their audiences. And yes, charisma can be developed or improved upon. I know and acknowledge that some people are naturally more charismatic than others, but that does not mean a less charismatic person cannot improve on their charisma. Let's just skip the preamble and head straight to how this can be done, shall we?

Engage Attention

You can tell when someone isn't given you their full attention, right? Perhaps they perceive you as boring? Or maybe you have not done enough to hold their attention. When you truly engage people's attention, they tend to stay glued to you and everything you have to say or present from start to finish. Great preachers, leaders, and musicians have this effect on their audiences. Here's how to engage attention:

1. Facial expression and gestures: what you say has more effect if there is an equally effective facial expression behind the words. Practice different facial expression with a close friend and ask for feedback. If you are not comfortable doing this in front of a friend, practice in front of a mirror. Use animated gestures too to give impact to your words.

2. Be present: if you truly want to engage someone's attention, put your devices on silent, keep them away or switch them off completely. The moment you begin to switch between humans and devices, you disengage from them. Also, remember to nod intermittently to show them you are present and listening.

3. Read emotions: play a video clip, preferably a clip you have not watched before, but mute the sound. I bet with a little bit of observation, you'll be able to figure what's happening in the clip. Now take that ability to observe with you as you step into social situations. By observing people's reactions you will be able to deduce unspoken cues and read their emotions.

4. Eye contact: the eyes have been said to be the window to the soul. When you look directly in the eye of whomever you are interacting with, you connect deeper with them. To create a sense of sincerity, competence, honesty, and confidence in your audience (individual or group) maintain eye contact with them for the most part of your interaction. Avoiding eye contact can seriously damage your charisma.

Affect Your Audience

Increase your charisma by influencing your audience in a powerful way. You really want to be perceived as a powerful and influential individual? Use these tips:

1. Confidence comes from knowledge: how well do you know what you know? How versatile and resourceful are you? And how many facts do you know about the things you know? You cannot come across as a confident person when your knowledge is very scanty. To boost your self-confidence, get to know a little about as many things as possible. Your self-confidence will definitely create an aura around you that influences people.

2. Pose: have you wondered why comical superheroes stand with their arms akimbo? It is a pose that conveys authority. Use poses that say "I'm in charge" to influence your audience. You can practice standing with both hands on your waist; or standing up, leaning forward and placing your hands on a table in front of you (very effective for showing authority in a meeting); or

you can place your hands at the back of your head while you lean far back into your chair (don't use this pose with your boss or in-laws!).

3. Poise: have poise; compose yourself. Have a controlled grace in your movements, gestures, and body language. Keep your hands still when talking. Don't fidget. Avoid excessive nodding. And keep away from too much speech hesitations such as uh... or um... verbal fillers indicate uncertainty and doubt – something you do not want to portray if you must improve your charisma.

4. Talk little: talking too much and rapidly is not a quality of an influential person. When you speak, talk unhurriedly. Make your words scarce and make them count. That way when you speak people know the value of your words and they listen.

James W. Williams

Making the Awkward Behavior Go Away

A lack of charisma tends to lead people to behave in a socially awkward manner. Imagine an upcoming musician with a great debut album standing on stage for the first time then fumbling with the microphone. He or she may have great talent but a poor charisma. When you feel out of place as you interact with friends, colleagues, or strangers, it makes you act oddly or clumsily. If that is the case, you need to improve your charisma to make the awkwardness go away. Here's how:

1. Socialize more: practice, they say, make perfect. Running away from places or situations that make you feel awkward will not make the awkwardness go away. You need to confront that fear by going to more social events. But do remember to go these events or gatherings with the aim of practicing how to interact with other people.

2. Stop worrying about your behavior: it's like this – the more your worry about being awkward, the more awkward you become. Relax. Be yourself. "But how can I be myself when I am awkward?" You are a work in progress so you are not awkward unless you label yourself that way. When you start believing that nothing can possibly go wrong in social situations, you give room for the best in you to blossom.

3. Fitness: what? Getting fit? Well, I know this may not be your typical charisma advice but look at this way. People who are overly worried about their physical looks tend to be too self-conscious during social interactions to think about charming people. In fact, they don't usually feel they have any charm in them. So yes, work on being fit (physical exercises, neat outward appearance, basic social etiquettes, etc) so you won't be bothered about inadequacies during social interactions.

Closing

Social skills are inescapable if you must enjoy the richness that life has to offer. Life does not happen in isolation; an abundance of friends and warm companions, great and new opportunities, and exciting life experiences do not happen to us when we back ourselves into obscurity because we lack the necessary social skills to explore life.

I have seen people miss out from life due to shyness, poor conversation skills, anxiety, and a plain lack of charisma. These are things this book has taken into consideration and offered tested suggestions on how to improve upon.

I encourage you to put to practice the techniques you have learned in this book. Don't be afraid or feel daunted by the idea of taking up a public speaking course. Heck, you can even practice in front of your mirror! Public speaking has a direct correlation on developing your social skills. Remember that you do not have to be a professional speaker or even aim to become one, to do this.

It is a wise practice to give a presentation every once in a while to sharpen your skills. You can volunteer to speak to your local youth to pass on some wisdom you have, or you can volunteer to teach your circle of friends something you are good at. While it is okay to form clear mental images in your mind and practice conversations in your head, it is equally important to form the habit of sharing who you are with the people around you. Don't just get good at explaining inside of your head. Let those around you get to actually hear you talk about the ideas in your head.

I'll not fail to mention that you may face rejection! But hey, that's a great way to improve your self-confidence. As you bounce back from rejection and seeming failure, you will get better at handling rejection.

One beautiful thing about stepping out and practicing what you have learned in this book is that it helps you improve on emoting; you get better at expressing your ideas and yourself. Suddenly, you no longer feel uncomfortable talking with people you don't know; a world of endless and limitless possibilities is laid bare before you. The world and the people in it become a familiar playground where you have absolute freedom to express your true and inner self.

Thank you!

Before you go, I just wanted to say thank you for purchasing my book.

You could have picked from dozens of other books on the same topic but you took a chance and chose this one.

So, a HUGE thanks to you for getting this book and for reading all the way to the end.

Now I wanted to ask you for a small favor. **Could you please consider posting a review on the platform? Reviews are one of the easiest ways to support the work of independent authors.**

This feedback will help me continue to write the type of books that will help you get the results you want. So if you enjoyed it, please let me know! (:

Lastly, don't forget to grab a copy of your Free Bonus book *"Bulletproof Confidence Checklist"*. If you want to learn how to overcome shyness and social anxiety and become more confident then this book is for you.

Just go to:

https://theartofmastery.com/confidence

www.ingramcontent.com/pod-product-compliance
Lightning Source LLC
Chambersburg PA
CBHW060034040426
42333CB00042B/2441